HOLINESS
The Fruit of the Spirit

CW01426107

Dr Alan C. Clifford

Grace & Truth

Text © The Publisher 2024

Layout © The Publisher 2024

First edition, Norwich Reformed Church, 2001

This edition first published in Great Britain 2024

by Charenton Reformed Publishing

https://english-reformed-church.co.uk/charenton-reformed-publishing/

ISBN 978-1-0686236-0-8 (pbk)

Typeset in Bookman Old Style (11 pt)

British Library Cataloguing in Publication Data.

A catalogue record for this book is available from the British Library.

Cover concept: A. C. Clifford, printed by Barkers Print & Design, Attleborough, Norfolk

Background cover picture: the author's beloved late wife Marian's blossoming new apple tree.

Contents

Introduction 5

1. Love 9

2. Joy 13

3. Peace 17

4. Long-suffering 21

5. Kindness 25

6. Goodness 29

7. Faithfulness 33

8. Gentleness 37

9. Self-control 41

10. The Benediction 45

Marian's fruit

HOLINESS
The Fruit of the Spirit

The fruit of the Spirit is love, joy, peace, long-suffering, kindness, goodness, faithfulness, gentleness, self-control. (Galatians 5:22-3)

Introduction

In these famous words, the Apostle Paul paints a portrait of Christian character. Believing in the Gospel of the Lord Jesus Christ and indwelt by the Holy Spirit of God, we present to others the evidence of God's saving work. By this means, God reveals Himself in us and through us, thus showing Himself to the world. Christian living is living proof of the living God. The kind of people we are should demonstrate that ruined and sinful mankind can only be transformed by God's power in Christ.

Becoming a Christian is to be transformed from our natural deformed state, so vividly outlined by Paul: 'Now the works of the flesh are evident, which are: adultery, fornication, uncleanness, licentiousness, idolatry, sorcery, hatred, contentions, jealousies, outbursts of wrath, selfish ambitions, dissensions, heresies, envy, murders, drunkenness, revels and the like' (Gal. 5:19-21). Together with a similar description in Romans 1:24-31, Paul's list mirrors the sin-sick and ungodly society of the ancient Graeco-Roman and modern worlds. This dark picture of human ugliness remains an exact portrayal of our state and condition. Apart from Christianity, all religions, philosophies and ideologies fail to make any significant impact upon our deformity. The advocates of culture, education and social policy are at best superficial, even assuming that they are in sympathy with Christian values—and many are not, even in the so-called Christian West! Only Jesus Christ can deliver us both from our wretchedness and the eternal judgement of God.

I. OUR HUMANITY: A CHRISTIAN VIEW

Over against the ugly deformity of sinful humanity is Paul's beautiful portrait of the Christian life. Describing 'visible' Christian character as 'fruit' implies the familiar picture of a tree. This is a frequently used biblical metaphor (see Ps. 1:3; Matt. 7:16-20). As fruit is evidence of a particular kind of tree, so there is more to Paul's picture than mere moral virtue and decency. Since only one kind of fruit grows on one variety of tree, Paul's 'tree' is obviously an unusual—and indeed miraculous—creation! This indicates that true Christians are 'walking miracles', a 'new creation' (2 Cor. 5:17). Before we examine the fruit in detail (during the subsequent nine studies), we will pursue the significance of the 'Christian tree'.

II. OUR ENVIRONMENT

As trees are located in a certain natural environment, so the Christian is placed in God's world. We should have a Christian 'world view'. Our sense of identity is based on God's self-revelation in creation, in the Scriptures and supremely in Jesus Christ. Paul refuses to view himself except from the perspective of Christ (Gal. 1:4; 4:9; 6:14). Thus we reject pagan, humanistic and materialistic cosmologies. The cosmic environment displays evidence of God's handiwork (see Ps. 19 and Rom. 1:19-20).

6

III. OUR IDENTITY

As trees have a definite identity, so the Christian view of ourselves is distinct from all others. Secular western thought is governed by *reductionism*. This comes in different forms. Some theorists reduce us to mere physics and chemistry. Some regard us a the products of biological evolution. Others view us as mere economic and social units, and so on. Since these outlooks tend to ignore our spiritual and ethical awareness, New Age mysticism is an over-reactionary but equally faulty alternative. The identity of the 'human tree' is derived from God's creative handiwork (Ps. 139). Our identity derives from creation 'in the image of God' (Gen. 1:27). Denying God's existence, wisdom and power, reductionists invent idols of their own as substitutes, e.g. science, philosophy and culture. Properly understood, these various perspectives are aspects only of that reality which proceeds from God. Fallen mankind has only a distorted view of human identity. The theory of evolution—a speculative scientific myth—is an example of how unenlightened people misread the data they try to interpret. Only through salvation in Christ do we 'rediscover ourselves'. Hence Paul only views his life in relation to Christ: 'the life which I live in the flesh, I live by faith in the Son of God, who loved me and gave himself for me' (Gal. 2:20). Paul explains the entire basis of his understanding more fully elsewhere (see Col. 1:13-20). Apart from the knowledge of God, all other knowledge is ultimately meaningless and useless. The knowledge of Christ is the key which unlocks all else.

IV. OUR ROOTS

As fruit derives ultimately from roots, so Christian fruit comes from Christian roots. Faith in God through Christ are the roots of a Christian. The ugly and distasteful fruit of sinful humanity is the product of the roots of a false faith. To deny God is to deny everything that is true, good and holy. When we trust in Christ crucified and raised from the dead for our salvation, we are justified (= forgiven and accepted) before a holy God. Such faith, formed by the knowledge of God's Word and confirmed in the sacraments, is nourished by the nutrients of God's grace, conveyed by the Holy Spirit. Thus faith 'works by love' (Gal. 5:6), transforming us into Christ's likeness. Fruit is the proof. We must beware of mere foliage, leaf without fruit. At best, false faith only produces a 'good showing in the flesh' (Gal. 6:12).

V. OUR SOIL

The soil in which we are planted is nothing other than the Lord Jesus Christ. We acknowledge Him as uniquely given by the Father (Gal. 4:4). True faith is rooted in this true soil, as false faith is rooted in false soil. Accordingly the fruit will indicate the root. We are either nourished in righteousness or wickedness. Hence Paul's vivid contrast between the 'works of the flesh' and the 'fruit of the Spirit'.

No other soil will save and sanctify like the Lord Jesus Christ. Our life and salvation comes only from Him. We cannot and do not give ourselves life and salvation. It is all of God's grace (Gal. 1:3,15). Hence Paul rejects any other pretended Gospel. Even if an angel from heaven, however eloquent and persuasive, offers a substitute faith, it is to be rejected (Gal. 1:8-9).

By examining the fruit in our lives, we will determine whether or not we are 'rooted in Christ' (Col. 2:6-7). If we discover ourselves to be 'fruitless', it is not too late to come to Christ in order to receive His life (Gal. 2:15-16).

1

..the fruit of the [Holy] Spirit is love...
(Gal. 5:22)

Introduction

Adding [Holy] to the text of Gal. 5:22 merely makes explicit what is surely implicit. The Apostle Paul is not speaking of some vague 'New Age' kind of spirit but the Holy Spirit of God, the third person of the Godhead. Consequently, the love which begins Paul's list is the divine love *agape*, not any kind of emotional disposition people might express. Indeed, we may say that *agape* was a New Testament Greek invention of the Holy Spirit to express all that is uniquely glorious about the love of God for mankind as revealed in His only-begotten Son (Jn. 3:16). *Agape* is therefore to be distinguished from *eros* (the usual Greek word for sexual love) and *phileo* (a general expression of tender affection).

The true meaning of *agape* must not therefore be lost among the popular ideas of love. For instance, the statue of Eros in London's Piccadilly Circus to celebrate the Earl of Shaftesbury's love for the poor was a monumental mistake! His philanthropy (love or *phileo* of man=*anthropos*) was motivated by *agape* not *eros*. Another vital point must be made. While it is fitting for Paul to commence with love since 'God is love' (1 Jn. 4:8), we must not be not be swayed by the popular sentimental misconception that God is exclusively love. Indeed, The Apostle John also reminds us that 'God is light' (1 Jn. 1:5). This demands the view that God's love is a holy love. While even *eros* has a God-given place within *married* love, homosexual acts are correctly viewed as perverted unholy love, despite the claims of so-called Christian Gay activists (see Rom. 1:24-7). Since God is the

God of truth (1 Jn. 5:6), love must never be an excuse for denying the truth (even though truth must be spoken with love, Eph. 4:15).

I. LOVE: THE FUNDAMENTAL

Here in Galatians 5, Paul is contrasting love with hatred (v.20). One is the fruit of the Spirit; the other is a work of the flesh. As if Paul was saying 'Nothing but evil comes from man; nothing good comes but from the Holy Spirit' (John Calvin). Elsewhere, Paul compares love with faith and hope (1 Cor. 13:13). While these three graces or fruit of the Spirit are necessary in this life, only love will be necessary in eternity. Faith and hope function now, but heaven will be 'a world of love' (Jonathan Edwards). The faith that brings us to Christ for pardon and the hope that leads us to heaven will have fulfilled their role. Love will be the totality of heavenly consciousness—love for God, for fellow-saints and the holy angels.

It is obvious why love is so fundamental. If God is love and we are made in God's image (Gen. 1:26-7), this explains the character of the Ten Commandments (Deut. 6:5; Lev. 19:18). The Lord Jesus Christ, filled with the Holy Spirit 'without measure' (Jn. 3:34), perfectly demonstrated the fruit of the Spirit. In Galatians, Paul is reminding us that through Christ and the power of the Holy Spirit, weak and frail believers are enabled to begin and anticipate the heavenly life. The heavenly state will demonstrate the perfect and completed work of God's grace declared in the Gospel. God's broken but satisfied Law will find full expression in heaven: God and neighbour will be loved without blemish or imperfection.

Our remaining sinful imperfection should constantly remind us of the fundamental importance of love. Battling against the world, the flesh and the devil, only the indwelling power of

10

God's love will preserve us against temptation. We must experience this 'expulsive power of a new affection' (Thomas Chalmers). The Bible shows us what can happen when love for God cools within us. Inevitably, love of the world takes over (1 Jn. 2:15-16). Kings David and Solomon were deceived by carnal love or lust when divine love was in decline (2 Sam. 11:3; 1 Kings 11:1). Beware of backsliding! Ananias and Sapphira (Acts 5:1-11) were clearly gripped by the love of money—*philarguria*. Paul lamented that 'Demas has forsaken me, having loved this present world' (2 Tim. 4:10). Is it any wonder that Christ warns us against 'covetousness' (Lk. 12:15-21)?

II. LOVE: THE COMMAND

Paul clearly taught that without the indwelling Spirit of God, it is impossible for us to love without *agape*. What enables us to love is 'the love of God [which] has been poured out in our hearts by the Holy Spirit' (Rom. 5:5). We cannot live as Christians without Christian life. Indeed, 'an empty sack cannot stand upright' (J. C. Ryle)! However, the grace of love never cancels the duty to love. Indeed, love is the fulfilling of the Law which still provides the agenda for the lover (Rom. 13:8-10).

However, our residual imperfection means that love might not always be felt. Yet the command to love remains (Jn. 15:12). We must not be governed by feelings or the lack of them! The demands of duty should drive us to prayer in order to think, feel and act as we should. The Lord will not fail us (Lk. 11:13). His grace will enable us to be dutiful. Our problems are chiefly to do with motivation. If we find it hard to love those who seem to us unlovely and unlovable, let us recall how God loves us. Did He not love the unlovely when He sent His Son (Jn. 3:16)? Are we attractive to Him because of our sin and rebellion? Hence when difficulties arise

11

among Christians (Eph. 4:31), the Gospel must be our guide: 'And be kind to one another, tender-hearted, forgiving one another, just as God in Christ also forgave you' (Eph. 4:32). '...he who loves God must love his brother also' (1 Jn. 4:21). Failure to do this is a complete denial of the Gospel. This comment about some early Christians has too often returned to haunt and humble us: "See how these Christians love one another! This surely reminds us that orthodoxy, church membership and moral character are nothing without the love of God. Christ asked penitent Peter not "Are you orthodox?" but 'Do you love me?' (Jn. 21:15-17). When we truly love Christ, we will then love each other 'fervently' (1 Pet. 1:22).

III. LOVE: THE DEMONSTRATION

Love among Christians is a powerful message to the world. Refrigerated orthodoxy will never warm a cold and loveless world. While love without truth is not Christian love, truth without love is not Christian truth! Theory and practice must go hand in hand. We should be 'walkers' as well as 'talkers' (1 Jn. 2:6). As Christ's lips and life spoke the same language, we should aim for the same consistency. Christian loving makes the love of God visible. Inward-working love will be outward-working love (1 Jn. 3:17; 4:20). Our love should be for believers and unbelievers alike (Gal. 6:10). We should show love and kindness to friends and foes, just as God does (Matt. 5:43-7). God's special love for His elect (Rom. 8:29-39) does not exclude His general love for the world (Jn. 3:16). May God give us grace to love as we are loved, to exhibit the fruit of the Spirit which is love, for the sake and glory of Him 'who loved us and gave Himself for us' (Gal. 2:20). Amen.

2

...the fruit of the [Holy] Spirit is...joy...
(Gal. 5:22)

Introduction

Joy of living (Fr. *joie de vivre*) is a basic human emotion. Life without joy is like a living death. Except for people in a suicidal state, it is rare for people not to rejoice in something or someone. As with the 'sister' grace of 'love', joy is either good or bad. As people sometimes love what is evil, so they delight or rejoice in evil (Prov. 2:14; 1 Cor. 13:6). Needless to say, Christians delight in what is good: they experience a 'holy joy'. If heaven is a 'world of love', it is also a realm of joy. 'In your presence is fulness of joy. At your right hand are pleasures for evermore' (Ps. 16:11). The Lord Jesus Christ speaks of 'joy in the presence of the angels of God over one sinner who repents' (Lk. 15:10). Such is the joy bestowed by the Holy Spirit of which Paul speaks in Gal. 5:22.

I. THE CONTEXT OF JOY

Paul is thus speaking particularly of the joy of a Christian. While we may possess common human joys in the order of God's providence—those of health, loving relationships, prosperity and the arts for instance, the distinctive joy of a Christian may exist when the others are in decline. An English Puritan soldier when dying of his battle wounds declared, "My joys far exceed all my pains! Christian joy comes from delighting in God and His grace revealed in the Gospel. Indeed, what we most delight in reveals what we most value. Music lovers delight most in music. Nature lovers delight most in wildlife and the countryside. Art lovers delight in great paintings. While Christians too may delight in music, art and nature, their supreme delight is always in God's love and mercy in Christ. In short, 'God lovers' delight most in God. Indeed, joy in God colours every other joy (although it can exist independently of them). Not without paradox, the Apostle Peter wrote of tried and troubled Christians rejoicing with 'joy inexpressible and full of glory' (1 Peter 1:6-8). Let us hear two hymn-writers:

Heaven above is softer blue,
Earth around is sweeter green,
Something lives in every hue,
Christless eyes have never seen;
Birds with gladder songs o'erflow,
Flowers with deeper beauties shine,
Since I know as now I know,
I am His and He is mine

George Robinson
(1838-77)

Object of my first desire,
Jesus crucified for me;
All to happiness aspire,
Only to be found in Thee:
Whilst I feel Thy love to me,
Every object teems with joy;
May I ever walk with Thee,
For 'tis bliss without alloy.

Augustus Montague Toplady
(1740-78)

II. THE CHARACTER OF JOY

The words of apostles and hymn writers should remind us that joyless Christianity is false Christianity. While Christians are not immune to sadness, such gloom and despondency are not the fruit of the Holy Spirit. They are the marks of sin and Satan. Although the Holy Spirit creates a consciousness of sin, it is intended only as a prelude to joy. Consequently, if Christian joy is to be a holy joy, then Christian holiness should be a joyful holiness. While English Puritanism has often been caricatured as miserable religion, there is no place for sour, glum Christians masquerading as holy Christians. That said, unbelievers often despise the joys of Christians. However, the feeling is mutual. Like Moses of old, true Christians choose 'rather to suffer affliction with

14

the people of God, than to enjoy the pleasures of sin for a season; esteeming the reproach of Christ greater riches than the treasures in Egypt' (Heb. 11:25-6). The immortal Puritan John Bunyan (1628-88) surely spoke for his and other generations of true Christians in *The Pilgrim's Progress* when, after Obstinate cried, "What... leave our friends and comforts behind us?", Christian replied: "Yes...because that ALL which you forsake is not worthy to be compared with a little of that which I am seeking to enjoy."

Christians are therefore not 'kill-joys". However, they have a serious joy as well as a holy joy. By comparison, the joys of unbelievers are trivial joys. How can things be otherwise unless joy is seen in the context of salvation? The oft-quoted words of the *Westminster Shorter Catechism* state that 'Man's chief end is to glorify God and to enjoy Him forever'. John Calvin (1509-64) declared that in view of the joy of salvation through Christ, 'Those who are not carried up above the heavens by this joy, so that they are content with Christ alone and despise the world, boast in vain that they have faith'. Calvin also reminds us that such a lofty view of joy has a very real human aspect to it. Indeed, it has a 'hilarious' character too: '[this joy is] that cheerfulness (hilaritas) towards our fellow-men, which is the opposite of moroseness'. Thus, before a laughing, joking world, in which comedians sometimes commit suicide, the hymn writer John Newton (1725-1807) wrote:

> Fading is the worldling's pleasure,
> All his boasted pomp and show;
> Solid joys and lasting treasure
> None but Zion's children know.

III. THE CREATION OF JOY

It is obvious that, as with any genuine joy, Christian joy is not self-induced. Sinful self-deception is not very convincing. Hence Paul says it is the 'fruit of the [Holy] Spirit'. It flows from His gracious work within us. It comes from the application of the truth of the Gospel to our hearts and lives. In short, only the Gospel can create true joy in God. The Gospel is 'good tidings of great joy' (Lk. 2:10). Thus we 'rejoice in God through our Lord Jesus Christ' (Rom. 5:11). True believers 'receive the Word with joy' (1 Thess. 1:6). The 'kingdom of God [within us] is…joy' (Rom. 14:17). Thus we have 'joy inexpressible' (1 Pet. 1:8). Indeed, it is God's gracious purpose that 'our joy may be full' (1 Jn. 1:4).

IV. THE DUTY OF JOY

While joy is graciously given to those who 'trust and obey'—for 'there's no other way to be happy in Jesus'—we are also commanded to rejoice (Philipp. 4:4). Even the often depressed psalmist could say 'I will rejoice in your salvation' (Ps. 9:14). If our feelings sometimes desert us, let us lift up our hearts to God. We are to be governed by facts rather than feelings. Feelings change, however desirable they are. Let us rest in God, remembering all that He has done for us. Depending on the Holy Spirit, we will again rejoice. Amen!

3

...the fruit of the [Holy] Spirit is...peace...
(Gal. 5:22)

Introduction

Peace is a precious and rare commodity in today's world. It
has been said that since the end of the second World War
the guns have not stopped firing, at least somewhere in the
world. None can deny that we live in a turbulent and vicious
world. Conflict and animosity—personal, domestic, religious
and political—are commonplace. The arms industries of the
world have plenty of customers. Despite high-powered
diplomatic activity by the UN and other agencies, the
human appetite for war seems unquenchable. Indeed,
popular TV and video entertainment suggests there is a
mass market for violence. Commerce makes much money
out of misery. People seem to love a fight. Our natural
propensities are evidently not peaceful.

King David lamented, 'I am for peace; but when I speak,
they are for war' (Ps. 120:7). The source of all our ills is, of
course, our fallen, sinful human nature. Our twisted and
self-centred wickedness means we are at war with God.
Thus '"There is no peace," says my God, "for the
wicked".' (Isa. 57:21), a text often partially quoted by
agitated people who seem quite untroubled about their
enmity to God (Rom. 8:7). The simple tragic fact is that our
broken 'vertical' relationship with God has consequences for
our 'horizontal' relationships with one another. Thus Paul
identifies 'hatred, contentions, jealousies, outbursts of
wrath...envy and murders' (Gal. 5:20-1). The only antidote
to these vicious tendencies and dispositions is the saving

17

and sanctifying work of the Holy Spirit. It is beyond the reach of mere civility and culture. In short 'peace' is 'the fruit of the [Holy] Spirit' (Gal. 5:22).

I. THE ROUTE TO PEACE

People who are far from God cannot know true peace. Gripped by sin and unbelief, unbelieving, lawless souls are restless. What little peace they might possess is easily disturbed by trying circumstances and unfriendly people. The peace of which Paul speaks we may 'contrast with quarrels and contentions' (Calvin). When this is experienced and enjoyed, we are less likely to be upset. the spiritual resources of this peace enable us to absorb the shock of quarrelsome and contentious people. Accordingly (in my own words),

How happy those who bring God's peace
To lives disturbed by sin;
They best can make all conflict cease
Who know that peace within.

The question is thus: how do we arrive at such peace? God's answer is the Gospel. Only when we recognise the fact of our spiritual hostility towards God is there any hope of peace. Since sin makes us enemies of God, our sin must be dealt with. Otherwise, no reconciliation, no peace. This is where the wonder of God's grace is seen (Jn. 3:16). The angelic message at Christ's birth was: 'Glory to God in the highest, and on earth peace, good will towards men!' (Lk. 2:14). Our Saviour entered the world as 'the Prince of peace' (Isa. 9:6). Since sin is the root cause of our alienation from God, Christ sacrificed His life and shed His blood to remove the barrier which makes us obnoxious to God? 'For Christ also suffered once for sins, the just for the unjust, that He might bring us to God' (1 Pet. 3:18). Thus 'made near by the blood of Christ,... He Himself is our peace' (Eph. 2:13-14). Christ has 'made

18

peace by the blood of His cross' (Col. 1:20). When we are alarmed by God's wrath, repenting of our sins and trusting Christ alone to save us, everything changes! 'Therefore, being justified by faith, we have peace with God through our Lord Jesus Christ' (Rom. 5:1).

II. PEACE WITH GOD

The objective ground of Christian peace in the Gospel is the basis of the subjective peace enjoyed by believers. The former produces the latter. The Holy Spirit works in us what Christ has done for us. The personal experience of peace with God then leads to peace enjoyed towards others, of which Paul speaks in Gal. 5:22.

It is important to know whether we possess a true peace or a false peace. The prophet warned against the deception of false peace: 'Woe to those who are at ease in Zion' (Amos 6:1). Even professing and backslidden Christians might have the peace of a cemetery. Thus it is necessary to be challenged. As has rightly been said, 'God is the disturber of the comfortable as well as the comforter of the disturbed'. Those who truly trust in Christ and 'walk in Him' (Col. 2:6) enjoy the peace of God subjectively. In our anxieties we may pray and feel 'the peace of God, which passes all understanding' (Philipp. 4:6-7) Like an 'umpire' in the soul, it is something better 'felt than telt'! Godly obedience is also involved in this: 'great peace have those who love your law' (Ps. 119:165).

The peace of God is independent of outward circumstances. It is more like the peace and security of chicks in a nest high on a cliff above the raging sea than the calm and tranquility of a quiet, rural scene. When he lay dying, the great English Reformed pastor Richard Baxter (1615-91) could say: "I have pain, there is no arguing against sense. But I have peace, I have peace!" The peace of God is the birthright of every true

Christian. We may enjoy 'righteousness, peace and joy in the Holy Spirit' (Rom. 14:17). In our daily warfare against 'the world, the flesh and the devil' our peace is often disturbed. Thus Paul reminds us that 'to be carnally minded is death, but to be spiritually minded is life and peace' (Rom. 8:6). Thus we need to be sanctified by 'the God of peace' (1 Thess. 5:23). Daily penitence and reliance on Christ, trusting in His gracious promises to pardon and purify us, is the way of regaining our subjective peace. However, nothing can change or remove the objective peace of Christ's finished work! On this sure foundation we must build day by day. Thus, at Christ's return, we are 'to be diligent to be found by Him in peace, without spot and blameless' (2 Pet. 3:14).

III. PEACE WITH OTHERS

This is what Paul is primarily concerned about in Gal. 5:22. Knowing the Holy Spirit's blessing enables us to show peace to others. Thus we are to 'pursue peace with all men' (Heb. 12:14). Our Lord said, 'Blessed are the peacemakers' (Matt. 5:9). While this never means 'peace at any price' (see Matt. 10:34-9), we will do everything in our power to promote peace with others. We will seek to take the heat out of conflict situations. We should be loving and friendly, ready when necessary to apologise—a sign of strength not weakness! Without compromising truth or convictions, we will seek peace and harmony. This is not always possible (Rom 12:18). If peace breaks down, let the fault be the other person's not ours. At peace with, and sanctified by, 'the God of peace' (Rom. 15:33; Heb. 13:20), we will then display the grace and character of Christ, 'Prince of peace'. May such fruit be evident in our lives. Amen.

4

...the fruit of the [Holy] Spirit is...long-suffering...
(Gal. 5:22)

Introduction

We need to be reminded that, in contrast to the 'works of the flesh' (v.19), the fruit of the spirit are what they are—the fruit of the Holy Spirit of God, produced in us by His power. The former are natural; the latter are supernatural. Paul is not describing natural virtues. Although seemingly-virtuous unbelievers might exhibit some of these dispositions temperamentally, only Christians born anew of the Spirit are able to demonstrate all of them. Even 'nice' unbelievers are who they are through God's gracious providence (or 'common grace'). In this sense, the vicious effects of fallen human nature are curbed and restrained (Matt. 5:46; Lk. 11:13; Rom. 5:7). Accordingly, while law, education and culture may produce virtuous people, only the saving grace of God can produce truly gracious people. As such, there is hope for the worst; we need not be perpetual victims of temperaments we are born with!

I. SOCIAL GRACE

When the fruit of the Spirit are spoken of, they are usually summed up by the first three—love, joy and peace'. Of course, the list includes the remaining six. Whereas the first three may be known as individual private states of mind and heart, 'long-suffering' instantly reminds us of the public aspect of our lives, viz. our relationships with others. In this sense, 'long-suffering' is not the same as 'patience' (as some Bible versions translate Paul's Gk: *makrothumia*, e.g. the NIV). While 'patience' may relate to situations and circumstances, 'long-suffering' always relates to other people. Thus Paul contrasts 'long-suffering' with 'outbursts of wrath' (v. 20). 'It characterises the person who, in relation to those who annoy, oppose, or molest him/her, exercises patience. He/she refuses to yield to passion or to outbursts of anger' (William Hendriksen).

From the context of Paul's Galatians, the public dimension to this fruit of the Spirit is clear. He is warning us against a selfish abuse of Christian liberty. Liberty in Christ is not freedom from law but from lawlessness (Gal. 5:13-14). Put differently, while we are delivered from the law's penal and condemning power (Gal. 3:13), we are not free from its preceptive and commanding power. It remains our duty to love God and our neighbour (v. 14). While this is impossible to fallen, unsanctified nature, it is possible to renewed, sanctified nature. Through the gracious working of the Holy Spirit, our duty may become our delight. Indeed, this is the only alternative to communities of people where short tempers are common: 'But if you bite and devour one another, beware lest you be consumed by one another!' (v. 15). In a word, 'long -suffering' is the gracious ability to be 'long tempered'. It specifies the way we should show Christ-like love to those who tend to provoke us. It is the public face of 'love' and 'peace', the antidote to 'hate' and 'contentions' (v. 20).

II. DIVINE GRACE

Notwithstanding the important distinction between 'long-suffering' and 'patience', the following 'kitchen prayer' has something to say to us at this point: "Lord, give me patience— but hurry!" We recognise therefore that only God can enable us to 'suffer long'. The question then becomes how to be long-suffering Christians. Indeed, how God trains His children to be Christ-like must be understood. It is not just the experience of a loving disposition. God teaches us by His Word as well as by His Spirit. In other words, as our knowledge of God's own character revealed in Scripture shows us how to love, we need to know about God's own 'long-suffering'.

If we are provoked into short-tempered outbursts towards others, imagine how we provoke God; our sins constantly provoke His holy wrath. But for His long-suffering, we would have no hope, in time or eternity. The amazing love of God towards a sinful world (Jn. 3:16) is revealed more fully by the way He 'puts up' with our persistent provocations. 'The Lord is gracious and full of compassion, slow to anger and great in mercy. The Lord is good to all, and his tender mercies are over all his works' (Ps. 145:8-9). God's long-suffering (Exod. 34:6) explains why Israel was not destroyed over the idolatry of the golden calf (Exod. 32). The Apostle Peter reminds us of God's long suffering towards the ungodly in Noah's day (1 Pet. 3:20), a kindness which shines even today through the Gospel (2 Pet. 3:9,15). The prophet Ezekiel highlighted God's long suffering towards rebellious Israel, showing that the Lord delighted more in saving them than destroying them (Ezek. 18:23ff). Paul himself pursues the same theme Rom. 9:22). In other words, God woos us with loving-kindness and tender mercy. He patiently bears with us that we might be saved. As Paul makes clear, this does not indicate some impotent waiting on God's part. While He waits, He calls us to repentance (Rom. 2:4). Not to turn from sin and to cease from provoking Him is to abuse His long-suffering and suffer His just judgement and wrath in the end. 'My Spirit shall not strive with man for ever' (Gen. 6:3).

The same long-suffering love was seen in the Lord Jesus Christ. Notwithstanding God's secret purpose sovereignly to gather His elect church (Jn. 6:37), the Lord Jesus still called rebellious Jerusalem to salvation (Lk. 13:34; 19:41). Our Saviour's long-suffering was general and indiscriminate. Christ's ambassador Paul showed the same disposition as he wrote to the Gentile people at Corinth (2 Cor. 5:9-21). While time is running out, we may understand that God's long-suffering is not yet exhausted! The Church must yet proclaim God's mercy while it lasts.

If God thus deals with us, how then should we deal with each other? In exactly the same way. We should be 'slow to wrath and quick to show mercy' (Col. 3:12). Understanding and experiencing the Gospel aright will therefore influence our relationships with others.

III. LIMITS TO GRACE

As Bible history makes clear, there are limits to God's long-suffering. His wrath against human sin will not be withheld forever. However long it seems delayed, Judgement Day is coming. This truth is mirrored in the question, is it ever wrong for us to be angry? Even the Lord Jesus showed righteous indignation when He cleansed the temple (Jn. 2:13 -17). Even Paul felt provoked by the idolatry at Athens (Acts 17:16). We too should be angry at human falsehood and wickedness (Ps. 4:4), especially our own; indeed, do we really show love when we are seemingly indifferent towards those who oppress and victimize others? In this sense, anger is an aspect of love. It is not love to tolerate everything! However, since righteous anger can easily become unrighteous anger, we must 'not let the sun go down upon our wrath' (Eph. 4:26). When all is said and done, our relationships with others must be dominated by God's long-suffering of us in Christ. The more we realise His mercy, it'll be easier to show mercy to others (Eph. 4:32). Amen.

5

..the fruit of the [Holy] Spirit is...kindness...
(Gal. 5:22)

Introduction

When we are in need, especially in a strange or foreign place, kindness is more precious than currency. A helping hand and a kind heart are beyond value. And yet, cruelty seems more common than kindness in many parts of the world. As cruelty is the offspring of hatred—a 'work of the flesh' (Gal. 5:20)—kindness is the offspring of love—both being the 'fruit of the [Holy] Spirit. The link with love illustrates another truth. Since love embraces our fellow human beings, so 'kindness' (Gk: *chrestotes*) is bound up with 'kind' (Gk: *genos*). A tender regard for other members of our 'kind' or 'race' is what kindness is all about.

At this point, synonyms can almost run into one another to the loss of their distinctive identity! Where the NKJV translates *chrestotes* as 'kindness', the AV rendering is 'gentleness'. However, the NKJV's 'gentleness' (v.23) comes from the Gk: *praotes* and is translated as 'meekness' in the AV! In 2 Cor. 10:1, the Apostle Paul unites *praotetos* with *epieikeias* when he refers to the 'meekness and gentleness of Christ' (AV and NKJV), where 'gentleness' suggests 'forbearance'—a not-too-distant 'cousin' of 'long-suffering' which we looked at in our previous study!

So, what are we talking about? For all the closeness of these rich words, the following should help eliminate any confusion:

a. kindness is a tender regard for others.

b. gentleness is a mild-mannered and generous spirit or 'sweet reasonableness' (M. Arnold).

c. forbearance is a desire to spare and a refusal to threaten.

d. long-suffering is a refusal to be impatient when we are provoked.

e. meekness is calmness of spirit and absence of self-assertiveness.

Clearly, all these 'graces' go together. Where there is kindness, there will also be gentleness, forbearance, long-suffering and meekness. To avoid too much overlap, we will confine ourselves to 'kindness and gentleness'.

I. KINDRED SPIRITS

Love for God and one another clearly implies kind hearts and gentle ways. Troubled and traumatised people in today's world were never in greater need of such love and consideration. Yet in our modern 'macho' world, these graces might easily be despised as weakness. The worlds of sport and film entertainment like heroes of sterner stuff! However, what applies to 'meekness' also applies to kindness and gentleness: 'If you think meekness is weakness, then try being meek for a week!'? A true story illustrates links gentleness and strength. In the Scottish highland games several years ago, a muscular man had just 'tossed the caber' (a roughly-hewn pine trunk). Suddenly, he noticed a small child crawling to where the caber was likely to land. With lightning reflexes, the man moved swiftly to snatch the child from danger just before the caber hit the ground. Kindness and gentleness combined with strength to avert a terrible tragedy. In like manner, King David could write of God's dealings with him: 'Your gentleness has made me great' (Ps. 18:35). So often, greatness goes with gentleness as smallness goes with snappishness. Little dogs usually bite whereas big ones lick you!

In the case of the highland sportsman, the child's deliverance might be viewed as 'kindness towards the innocent'. As with all the fruit of the Spirit, they specify how undeserving, saved sinners should behave towards other undeserving, saved sinners. King David's life illustrates this in two vivid cases which also depict God's gracious dealings with us:

1. *Kindness for the guilty.* God's judgement upon David for his sins of adultery and complicity in murder involved the insurrection of his son Absalom. When the tide turned in the king's favour and Absalom was being hunted, David pleaded: "Deal gently for my sake with the young man Absalom." (2 Sam. 18:5). On hearing of his death, David cried, "O my son Absalom—my son, my son Absalom—if only I had died in your place! O Absalom, my son, my son!" (v.33). Revenge found no place in David's soul. Indeed, 'Kindness [is] nobler ever than revenge' (Shakespeare, *Two Gentlemen of Verona*). Is there not in this a reflection of God's kindness towards the ungodly upon whom His wrath nonetheless falls? The great English Puritan John Howe (1630-1705) expressed this in his famous sermon *The Redeemer's Tears Wept over Lost Souls:* 'You will not perish unlamented, even with the purest, heavenly pity'. Truly, God 'has no pleasure in the death of one who dies' but 'that he should turn from his ways and live' (Ezek. 18:23, 32).

2. *Kindness for the needy.* After David was established on his throne, his energies and attentions were turned in more conciliatory directions. So he asked: "Is there still anyone who is left of the house of Saul, that I may show him kindness for Jonathan's sake?" (2 Sam. 9:1). More

27

pointedly, David desired to show 'the kindness of God' (v.3). When the king learned of Jonathan's lame son Mephibosheth, he ordered that the cripple should appear before him "to eat bread at my table continually" (v.7). Thus summoned by kindness, and illustrating our true response to the lovingkindness of the Lord, Mephibosheth said, "What is your servant, that you should look upon such a dead dog as I? Thus, as sinners are treated as children of God (1 Jn. 3:1), the favoured cripple was called by David to "eat at my table like one of the king's sons." (v.11).

II. A KINDRED GOD

The ultimate demonstration of kindness is the Gospel. 'But when the kindness and the love of God our Saviour towards man appeared...' (Titus 3:4). While God is our creator, yet through the incarnation of His only-begotten Son (Jn. 3:16), He became in a profound sense 'one of us'. As Athanasius (c. 296-373) elegantly expressed it: 'The Son of God became the Son of Man, so that the sons of men may become sons of God'.

God's good and gracious gifts are gifts of loving-kindness (Ps. 103:4). This is a famous Old Testament theme which comes to its fullness in CHRIST through 'the tender mercy of our God' (Lk. 1:78). Forgiveness of sins, spiritual new birth, the assurance of salvation, sanctifying and sustaining grace and everlasting life and glory—all these are the gifts of God's undeserved kindness. If God has shown such kindness to us, should we not show kindness to others, and especially to those 'who are of the household of faith' (Gal. 6:10)? Since Christ is gentle towards us (2 Cor. 10:1; Isa. 40:11), we should be kind and gentle towards each other. This is a lesson for pastors in particular (1 Thess. 2:7; 2 Tim. 2:24) and Christians in general (Jas. 3:17). May the Holy Spirit make us gentle and kind. Amen.

6

..the fruit of the [Holy] Spirit is...goodness...
(Gal. 5:22)

Introduction

The Apostle Paul now highlights an obvious contrast between the 'works of the flesh' (v.19) and the 'fruit of the Spirit'. Whereas God's nature and activities are 'good', human nature and activities are—apart from God's power and grace—all 'bad'. By implication, Paul is challenging the idea of natural human goodness, a view occasionally affirmed by some romantic idealists. Indeed, according to the Bible, human nature is 'totally depraved', not in the sense that everyone is as outwardly bad as they could be but that no faculty or feature of human personality remains unaffected by sin. We may argue that wherever goodness is found, even in the lives of non-Christians, this is to be attributed to God. His providence—through education, culture and legal/social constraints—prevents the naturally bad inclinations of human nature finding full expression in every situation. When terrible things do happen, we are reminded of the ugly potential for 'badness' we all possess. Christians therefore acknowledge that, in a special saving sense and degree, 'all that is good in us is from God in us'. To coin a saying, 'true goodliness comes from true godliness'.

I. THE NATURE OF GOODNESS

'Goodness' is one of the 'communicable attributes' or excellencies of God. When He brings us into communion with Himself through His grace revealed in Christ, He imparts His own goodness to us. We thus have an appetite for goodness when we have an appetite for God (Matt. 5:6). Not until we are firmly persuaded that 'badness' reigns within us until God unites us to Himself, will we seek goodness in Him alone. Elsewhere Paul reminds us of the ugly truth that there is—naturally speaking—'no one that does good, no not one' (Rom. 3:12 quoting Pss. 14:1-3; 53:1-3; Eccl. 7:20). Speaking more personally, he lamented that 'in me dwells no good thing' (Rom. 7:18). Aristotle's definition is therefore flawed despite its noble and idealistic rhetoric: 'It is thought that every activity, artistic or scientific, in fact, every deliberate action or pursuit has for its object the attainment of some good. We may therefore assent to the view...that "the good" is "that at which all things aim"'(*Ethics* I:1). Whereas this ought to be the case prescriptively, sinful human nature has the tendency, speaking descriptively, to aim at what is bad with unerring accuracy! The only exceptions are due to the providence of God, for which He alone should receive the credit.

In a sense, 'goodness' is almost as indefinable as God is. It is not quite the same as 'righteous'. Like the word 'love', the English 'good' translates several Greek words and is best grasped as an adjective rather than a noun, e.g. *Agathos* is the character of something or someone. In a moral sense, God is supremely—even exclusively, according to Jesus—good (Mk. 10:18). He is thus the absolute standard of goodness. *Kalos* denotes what is intrinsically good or beautiful and is used with reference to fruit (Matt. 3:10), ground (Matt. 13:8), God's law (Rom. 7:16) and faithful ministers of Christ (1 Tim. 4:6). *Chrestos* is said of pleasant things and gracious people (1 Cor. 15:33; Rom. 2:4). The noun *agathosune* is used to describe the moral quality of true Christian or regenerate people (as here in Gal. 5:22). In short, our goodness derives directly from God's Holy Spirit (see Ps. 143:10).

All goodness therefore derives from God. His kindness, mercy, grace and love are all comprehended in Ps. 145:9: 'The Lord is gracious and full of compassion, slow to anger and great in mercy. The Lord is good to all, and his tender mercies are over all his works'. This we may call God's common grace or goodness. However, towards the church of His elect people, God exercises a special grace: 'Truly God is good to Israel' (Ps. 73:1; Gal. 6:16). Nonetheless, in the preaching of the Gospel, God 'commands all men everywhere to repent' (Acts 17:30) and God's gracious long-suffering in Christ towards a guilty, sinful world is described by Paul as 'the goodness of God' which 'leads you to repentance' (Rom. 2:4). Thus the good news of the Gospel is: 'Oh, taste and see that the Lord is good; blessed is the man who trusts in him' (Ps. 34:8).

When the Lord Jesus asked the rich young ruler, "Why do you call me good? No one is good but one, that is God" (Mk. 10:18), He was not denying that He was God the Son incarnate and consequently a partaker of His Father's divine goodness, but only challenging the young man's perception of Christ. Accordingly, in the highest possible divine sense, it was said of Christ that He 'went about doing good' (Acts 10:38). Bearing in mind what is true of the Holy Spirit (see Ps. 143:10), 'goodness' is that excellence and perfection of nature possessed by the triune God.

II. THE NURTURE OF GOODNESS

Goodness is something Christians should obviously delight in. 'He has shown you, O man, what is good; And what does the Lord require of you but to do justly, to love mercy, and to walk humbly with your God' (Mic. 6:8). Like our Lord, we should be in the best possible sense 'do gooders'! Indeed, God's predestinating purpose is to make us like Christ (Rom. 8:29). By reminding us that 'goodness' is a fruit of the Spirit, Paul thus teaches us that God's intention is to reproduce His nature in us (see 2 Pet. 1:4). The wonder of the Gospel is that naturally bad people can be made good. Thus God-given goodness has two parts. First, when we trust Him for salvation, Christ declares us good by pardoning our sins through His blood and thus washing away the badness of our guilt (justification). Second, He begins to make us good by giving us His Holy Spirit (sanctification). This is where pagan Aristotle got it wrong! He taught that a person does good in order to become good. The Gospel teaches us that once a person becomes good— through God's grace not our merit—then he will do good. Our goodness always remains imperfect in this life hence we always need pardon for our best endeavours.

A true Christian therefore has an appetite for goodness. With minds transformed by Christ we will 'prove what is that good and acceptable and perfect will of God' (Rom. 12:2). We will 'meditate' on things 'noble, just, pure, lovely and good' (Philipp. 4:8). Indeed, we will 'always pursue what is good' and 'hold fast what is good' (1 Thess. 5:15, 21). Consequently, a Christian will delight in 'good works' which are the undeniable fruit of a true, living and justifying faith (Eph. 2:8-10). Thus 'good works' are the outward expression of an inward goodness which is the fruit of the Spirit.

Since temptations to 'badness' gives us no rest through 'the world, the flesh and the devil', goodness requires constant nurture. Since God communicates His goodness through word and sacrament by His Holy Spirit, we must be diligent in private and public worship. We must constantly hear the good Word of God. We must be filled with the Spirit of God. We must pray for the sense of the love of God (Jude 20-21). We must seek fellowship with the people of God. Then, greater 'godliness' will produce greater 'goodliness' (Jude 24-5). Amen.

7

..the fruit of the [Holy] Spirit is...faithfulness...
(Gal. 5:22)

Introduction

Having spoken of three private or 'inward' fruit (love, joy, peace) and three public or 'outward' fruit (long-suffering, kindness and goodness), Paul now touches on the vital relationship between these two 'trios'. In other words, our thinking and loving should be sincerely seen in our speaking and acting. In short, we should be people of fidelity. A faithful correspondence or likeness should exist between what we profess and what we are.

I. SCRIPTURAL FIDELITY

Paul is not speaking simply of saving faith in Christ (as the English AV (1611) might suggest), although this is foundational to faithfulness in its widest sense. Later commentators made this clear. Matthew Henry says Paul writes of 'fidelity, justice and honesty in what we profess and promise to others'. Philip Doddridge wrote that 'The Spirit of truth...leads us most strictly to observe fidelity, or good faith and uprightness in all our dealings...[without] failing in any of those engagements which it is in our power to fulfil'. More recently Frederic Rendell stated: 'It is clear from the subordinate place assigned to [faith] *pistis* (Gk) that it does not here denote the cardinal grace of faith in God which is the root of all religion, but rather good faith in dealing with men, and due regard to their just claims'.

II. HIGH FIDELITY

There is a timely ring about Paul's teaching. In days when 'image' is all too important, there is a credibility gap between promise and performance. People meaning what they say is essential for harmonious relationships in society. According to Paul, religious apostasy or 'ungodliness' produces moral and social chaos or 'unrighteousness' (Rom. 1:17). In the earlier decades of the electronic revolution, the advance from the old 78 rpm records to the 33.33 rpm LPs introduced us to 'hi-fi' or high-fidelity sound reproduction. At a time of religious decline, this 'sixties' technological revolution was matched by rising marital infidelity. The advent of CDs and computers has seen increasing music 'hi-fi' but rising moral 'low-fi'! During this period, the Christian church has not been immune from these influences. Clearly, the New Testament churches could not ignore these problems either. In every age, Christians must aim for 'hi-fi' spirituality. This is all about being consistent and genuine in every apect of life. Hypocrisy will be hateful to us as we seek to be real and true Christians. Paul is obviously contrasting 'faithfulness' with such 'works of the flesh' (v.19) as adultery (infidelity towards one's spouse), idolatry (infidelity towards God), hatred - and murder? - (infidelity towards our fellow human beings) and heresies (infidelity towards God's truth). In speaking of the fruit of the Holy Spirit, Paul is reminding us that until and unless God makes us faithful Christians we are by nature faithless sinners. Even with the Lord's enabling, we will always fall short. Yet progress may be made, and should be made, however small.

III. CHRISTIAN FIDELITY

Only the Holy Spirit can grant us deep convictions about spiritual fidelity. After all, He is 'the Spirit of truth' (Jn. 15:26). He is who He is—'proceeding from the Father'—

because 'God is true' (Rom. 3:4). Accordingly, the Bible, inspired by God (2 Tim. 3:16) must be true, reliable, trustworthy and inerrant (2 Pet. 1:16-21). Holy Scripture bears faithful witness to Christ who is '...the truth...' (Jn. 14:6).

Therefore, Christians will be people of truth and fidelity. They will seek to be:

1. Faithful to the Scriptures in doctrine and practice (Gal. 1:6-12).

2. Faithful to Christ in serving Him with a loving and obedient faith (Gal. 1:10; 5:6).

3. Faithful to fellow Christians in general and church-members in particular (Gal. 6:1-5).

4. Faithful in speaking the truth and in keeping confidences (Gal. 4:16; 2:2).

5. Faithful to their spouses (where applicable) in thought, word and deed (Gal. 5:19; 6:8).

6. Faithful in word and deed to neighbours and others in society (Gal. 6:10).

7. Faithful in persevering despite discouragements (Gal. 6:9).

IV. DIVINE FIDELITY

God not only enables us to be faithful Christians through the energy of His Holy Spirit. He also teaches and encourages by example. Consider Him therefore:

'Through the Lord's mercies we are not consumed, because His compassions fail not. They are new every morning; great is your faithfulness" (Lam. 3:23).

'Your mercy, O Lord, is in the heavens, and your faithfulness reaches to the clouds' (Ps. 36:5).

'If [David's sons] forsake my law...If they break my statutes...Nevertheless my loving-kindness I will not utterly take from [them], nor allow my faithfulness to fail' (Ps. 89:30-33).

Since 'all the promises of God in [Christ] are 'Yes' and 'Amen' (2 Cor. 1:20), we may be sure that God is faithful to His word, especially to His promises of grace.

Therefore we may trust Him faithfully to:

1. Receive us when we seek Him (Matt. 11:28; Jn. 6:37).

2. Pardon us when we confess our sin and guilt (1 Jn. 1:9; Heb. 10:19-23).

3. Sanctify us and prepare us for everlasting glory (1 Thess. 5:23).

4. Keep us by His grace and be with us (Matt. 28:20; 1 Pet. 1:5).

Convicted of our faithlessness and frequent infidelities, let us despair of ourselves but be confident in God. Through our example and testimony, others will see God's fidelity! Amen.

8

..the fruit of the [Holy] Spirit is...gentleness (or meekness)...
(Gal. 5:23)

Introduction

Having specified the link of fidelity or faithfulness between the three private or inward fruit (love, joy and peace) and the three public or outward fruit (long-suffering, kindness and goodness), Paul concludes with two requirements of order, viz. meekness and self-control. The sinful 'works of the flesh' (v.22) always produce pride and confusion in human life. Meekness (or gentleness) is the first antidote to the destructive disorder of human sin.

Paul reminds us that only God can deliver us from ourselves. Meekness is a fruit of the Holy Spirit not something natural. Pride is our great enemy and yet how blind we are to its influence! Indeed, the great achievers of this world—in sport, politics and business—are usually strong-minded, assertive people. They are 'pushy' and ambitious. They manipulate or 'push around' other people to get their own way. Such people always 'aim for the top', for wealth, power and importance. They get talked about and become famous. Meekness is never commended by pagan Greek and Roman writers who always preferred the self-confident, assertive kind of man. Ever since God was dethroned in the human soul, we all have the tendency to become tyrants.

I. THE MEANING OF MEEKNESS

Our meek Redeemer says meekness is a primary quality of a true Christian (Matt. 5:5). Without it, the proud and the powerful will lose everything they ever possessed. With it,

Christians will 'inherit the earth'. If meekness is too rare, it is also rarely understood correctly. It does not describe a retiring, quiet kind of individual. Being 'meek' is not being casual, easy-going and 'laid back'. Neither does it mean being pleasant and 'nice'. It certainly doesn't describe people of weak personality or character. Moses was a man of great strength but he is described as 'meek' (Numb. 12:3). Was the 'meek' (Matt. 11:29) Lord Jesus Christ weak (Jn. 2:15)? Someone has written: 'if you think meekness is weakness then try being meek for a week!'

Meekness may be defined as having a quiet, humble, dependent and teachable spirit, with total trust in God (Matt. 6:33) despite all unpleasant and irritating provocations (Matt. 5:44). Christ's true disciples meekly accept His word (Jn. 14:23). In the Old Testament, 'meekness' basically means a state of poverty and affliction from which the idea of patient submission is derived (Ps. 10:12-18). In the New Testament, 'meekness' is an inward attitude implying a gentle and non-aggressive disposition, seen especially in CHRIST (2 Cor. 10:1).

II. THE MANNER OF MEEKNESS

Meekness may be viewed from three aspects:

1. With reference to God, meekness is 'resignation and submission':

a. We become amazed that God is so gracious to us (Eph. 2:1-5).

b. We are patient under trials as Job was: 'The Lord gave and the Lord has taken away' (Job. 1:21).

c. We realise that we are always in God's debt (Matt. 6:12).

He owes us nothing.

2. With reference to others, meekness is 'mildness and gentleness':

a. We regard ourselves as less worthy than others (Phil. 2:3b).

b. We are not proud and boastful (1 Cor. 13:4; Phil. 2:3a).

c. We are not sensitive and defensive (1 Cor. 13:5; Jas. 3:17).

d. We are not inclined to retaliate under criticism (1 Pet. 2:23).

e. We are amazed when others think well of us (2 Sam. 9:8).

3. With reference to ourselves, meekness means 'patience and contentment':

a. We are content and satisfied with God's provision and dealings with us (Phil. 4:11).

b. We realise that future glory outweighs present trials and deprivations (2 Cor. 4:16-18).

III. MEN OF MEEKNESS

How do our lives reflect the spiritual quality of meekness? Abstract characteristics are better portrayed in living examples. Moses (Numb. 12:1-3) and David (2 Sam. 16:11) were submissive to God while under criticism. Paul urges meekness in rebuking an erring brother (2 Tim. 2:25). He patterned his own behaviour with the Corinthian church on Christ's meekness (2 Cor. 10:1-18). Peter urges meekness in arguing with unbelievers (1 Pet. 3:15). The supreme example is therefore the Lord Jesus Himself. He was meekness without parallel before His accusers (1 Pet. 2:21-3).

IV. THE MAKING OF MEEKNESS

How can we become meek? God's word directs us accordingly:

1. Only by His grace. It is a spiritual grace (Gal. 5:23) not a natural art.

2. Only by personal union with Christ. He teaches us in the course of a life-long personal relationship with Him (see Matt. 11:28-30). 'Yoked together' with Him, he alone can subdue our turbulent, restless self will.

3. Only by regular, daily repentance and faith. Our spiritual warfare is a succession of failure, recovery, pardon and gradual progress (2 Pet. 3:18). The ultimate victory is certain (see Jude 24-5).

CONCLUSION

Total surrender to God's grace and power will ensure meekness. Resistance and rebellion can only hinder it. Relying upon Christ, the 'root' will produce the 'fruit'. May we be always rooted in Him (Jn. 15:1-8).

9

..the fruit of the [Holy] Spirit is...self-control...
(Gal. 5:23)

Introduction

In permissive Western society, we often hear calls for 'self-discipline' and 'self-regulation', especially in sexual ethics, schools and other areas of public life. We are frequently told that personal and public morality are two distinct things. However, with no agreement over objective standards of morality in a post-Christian era, personal relativism can easily lead to public chaos. What can fill the moral vacuum? Humanism? Islam? Totalitarian regimes?

Self-discipline implies not only recognised standards but the character and ability to observe them. As we need a highway code on public roads and regulations governing public hygiene, etc., so self-control for sinful human nature requires the God-given context of Law and Gospel. Society cannot therefore rely on subjective standards and self-help resources. When he considers 'self-control', Paul assumes the validity of the Judeo-Christian context.

I. SELF-CONTROL IS DIVINE CONTROL

Meekness (or gentleness) involves our voluntary submission and resignation to God. In short, we surrender ourselves to His control. However, this is not fatalism: God does not govern us like blocks of wood; we still retain our personal identity and accountability. Liberated by His grace, our 'higher' or new nature is to control our 'lower' or old nature. Brought under the divine discipline of the Holy Spirit, we also discipline ourselves. With His aid we take God's side against ourselves: thus we exhibit the 'fruit of the Spirit' rather than the 'works of the flesh' (v.19).

Therefore, the Holy Spirit's work does not exclude effort on our part. Sanctification clearly has an active as well as a passive aspect. In this inward spiritual conflict, we bring 'every thought into captivity to the obedience of Christ' (2 Cor. 10:5). As long as our earthly warfare lasts, we need divine resources to master ourselves (Eph. 6:10-18). As we cannot save ourselves, so we cannot control ourselves without the Holy Spirit. We are to 'work out' (or 'out-work') our salvation precisely because God is working is us (Philip. 2:12-13). God works, we work! We apply what He supplies. This is the secret of self-government. Accordingly, 'the person who is blessed with this quality possesses 'the power to keep himself in check', which is the meaning of the word in the original' (William Hendriksen).

II. SELF-CONTROL AND THE LORDSHIP OF CHRIST

As discipline derives from discipleship, so Paul is implying total submission to Christ. He is the Church's prophet, priest and king. As prophet He teaches us by His Word and Spirit. As priest He has satisfied for our sins and now intercedes for us before the Father. As king, He saves, protects, guides and rules us. Self-control is not possible unless Christ controls us entirely. 'Christ will not save whom He doesn't rule' (Matthew Henry).

Thus true faith (a) assents to Christ's teaching (the entire Bible), (b) trusts heartily and exclusively in the merit of His sacrifice, and (c) obeys gladly His lordship and authority (Rom. 6:17). Only then will the divine resources be available for us to control ourselves. Christ mediates His power to our souls, thus enabling us to govern ourselves by His power (Jn. 15:5; Philip. 4:13).

III. SELF-CONTROL IS FOR OUR WHOLE BEING

a. Our thoughts are to be brought to the obedience of Christ (2 Cor. 10:5).

b. Our tongues are to be 'bridled' and 'tamed' by the word and power of God (Jas. 3:1-12)

c. Our emotions are to be subject to the spirit of Christ (2 Tim. 1:7).

d. Our wills are to be subject to God's will (Matt. 6:10).

e. Our bodies must be disciplined as soundly as our souls (1 Cor. 9:27).

IV. SELF-CONTROL IS GROWTH CONTROL

As with all the fruit of the Spirit, self-control is never perfect in this life. Gradual growth is the process. As 'Rome was not built in a day', neither is Christian character completed in a sudden flash of sanctification. Guarding against both complacency and despair, God calls us to make progress day by day. Pardon is available for our failures and falls; more grace is available to get up again and continue. In short, we are to grow in grace (2 Pet. 3:18). Our encouragement is that God will complete the work He has begun in us (Philip. 1:6), keeping us by His grace and power (1 Pet. 1:5). He is able to 'present us faultless' at last (Jude 24-5)!

Since personal government involves both divine discipline and self discipline, it all depends on our personal relationship with Christ. This truth is best illustrated by our Saviour Himself in His great Gospel invitation (Matt. 11:28-30). We note the following features:

43

1. THE INVITATION: *'Come to me':*

Like wild young oxen, turbulent, self-willed and rebellious sinners are welcomed by Christ. The restless chaos of our sin-wrecked lives will be replaced by the 'rest' of pardon and peace.

2. THE COMMAND: *'Take my yoke upon you':*

Christ is Lord as well as Saviour. We must submit in order to receive the blessing. The young ox must place its neck in the yoke and be led and instructed by Christ. The young ox surrenders to the mature ox. Only then will we 'learn' the secret of pulling the plough. Such are the duties of prayer, Bible reading, worship, self-examination and all aspects of practical godliness.

3. THE PROMISE: *'You will find rest to your souls':*

Christ knows our weakness and frailty. He was tempted as we are. He is a gentle and kind Lord. Unlike the yokes of the devil and human masters, Christ's is 'lined with love and padded with peace' (v.29). When we surrender to His government, we begin to govern ourselves aright. Then we know rest. Once begun in this life, we will then enjoy eternal rest in heaven.

10

THE BENEDICTION

*'The grace of our Lord Jesus Christ, and the love of God,
and the communion of the Holy Spirit be with you all. Amen.'*
(2 Corinthians 13: 14)

Introduction

The pursuit of holiness must be seen in the context of our understanding *and* experience of Trinitarian grace—grace that pardons *and* purifies. Since the problems facing the Galatian churches also troubled the church at Corinth, Paul's teaching to the latter provides a relevant and useful conclusion to our 'Growing in Grace' series. His benediction or 'blessing' is an important liturgical element in New Testament worship. Other examples might be Ephesians 3: 20-1 and Jude 24-5. Following the Trinitarian style of the baptismal formula in Matthew 28: 19, Paul's benediction probably reflects also the high priestly blessing of Numbers 6: 24-6:

The LORD bless you and keep you;
The LORD make his face shine upon you,
and be gracious unto you;
The LORD lift up his countenance upon you,
and give you peace.

The beautiful words of this famous 'triple' blessing provide clear Old Testament evidence for Trinitarian truth. Needless to say, such truth is scattered throughout the New Testament. Thus Charles Hodge wrote of Paul's benediction: 'The distinct personality and the divinity of the Son, the Father, and the Holy Spirit, to each of whom prayer is addressed, is here taken for granted. And therefore this passage is a clear recognition of the doctrine of the Trinity, which is the fundamental doctrine of Christianity. For a Christian is one who seeks and enjoys the grace of the Lord Jesus, the love of God [the Father], and the communion of the Holy Ghost.'

Indeed, no truth is more fundamental or practical. To the Israelite of old and the Christian alike, having the blessing of God is the crowning mercy of life. So Daniel Mayo wrote that 'we can desire no more to make us happy than the grace of Christ, the love of God, and the communion of the Holy Ghost.' Without it, all other blessings are but curses. Enjoying the blessing of God ensures that His other gifts are sanctified and enjoyed without guilt and with a peaceful conscience. Thus the benediction also serves as a daily practical corrective for us. If we cannot with a comfortable conscience enjoy what we consider desirable, then we are better off without it, however appealing and attractive it might otherwise seem. Whatever displeases the LORD must not please His people.

A question might arise concerning the order of Paul's words. "Surely," someone asks, "should not the love of the Father come before the grace of the Son, as in the baptismal formula?" One answer could be that a rigid *theological* order is not always observed. True, we think of the three persons of the Godhead in the 'natural' order of Father, Son and Holy Spirit: the Father has begotten the Son, and the Son sends the Spirit who proceeds from the Father. However, if all three persons are *eternal*, we ought not to suggest that a fixed verbal order reflects *temporal* distinctions which do not exist.

While it is helpful to see the 'Father, Son, Spirit' pattern of Matthew 28: 19 in the order of salvation stated by Paul elsewhere *(see Eph. 1: 1-13),* there is probably a good reason why he uses a different order in 2 Corinthians 13: 14. While the usual form states the order of salvation from *God's side* (see also *Jn. 3: 16)*, the benediction states things from *our side*. We only have confidence in drawing near to God because we approach Him through Christ. Thus John Calvin wrote:

> For God, as far as He Himself is concerned, loved us from before the foundation of the world and redeemed us solely because He loved us, but we, when we look at ourselves, see nothing but sin which provokes wrath, and we cannot grasp God's love without a mediator. Thus, as far as we are concerned, Christ's grace is the beginning of God's love.

In other words, when we first fix the eye of faith on the Lord Jesus, we become more persuaded of God the Father's love, as Charles Wesley shows:

O God of all grace,
Thy goodness we praise;
Thy Son Thou hast given to die in our place.
He came from above
Our curse to remove;
He hath loved, He hath loved us, because He would love.

In view of the varieties of wickedness Paul had to expose in the Corinthian and Galatian churches *(see 1 Cor. 6: 9-11; 2 Cor. 12: 21; Gal. 5: 19-21)*, he very likely wished to emphasise God's great willingness to forgive them when they repented *(see 2 Cor. 7: 10-12)*. This truth should encourage us also, since the devil is happy if he can cause us to despair of finding God's mercy. We should remember that 'Christ Jesus came into the world to save *sinners*' *(1 Tim. 1: 15)*.

1. THE GRACE OF THE SON

Since it is impossible to draw near to God without the mediation of Christ, we must be persuaded that He is the only way to the Father *(see Jn. 14: 6; 1 Tim. 2: 5)*. God's favour can only be received by guilty sinners through Christ our sin-bearer. We are 'justified by His blood' *(Rom. 5: 9)*. To deny the necessity of Christ's priestly mediation is either to imagine we are not sinners or that God's holiness is no threat. This is the error of every religion that denies the person and work of Christ. Since we are sinful, the willingness of Christ to receive us and save us appears all the more wonderful. The self-righteous Pharisees failed to understand that 'This man receives *sinners*' *(see Mk. 2: 1-17)*. This however is the great wonder of the Gospel! The more conscious we are of our sins, the more hope there is for us, if only we renounce and reject them, and trust in the Lord Jesus.

2. THE LOVE OF THE FATHER

Once we have come to the Son, we discover that the Father loved us all the time! Without Christ we are only certain of God's wrath. It is also presumptuous to imagine that the Father will receive us if we reject and despise the mediation of the Son. Those alone honour the Father who honour the Son *(see Jn. 5: 23)*. However great our sins might be, if we trust only in the sacrifice of Christ—salvation is by God's mercy not our merit —we may be assured that the Father 'sees us and has compassion, and runs and falls on our necks and kisses us' *(Lk. 15: 20)*. Thus, with the Son and the Spirit, the Father delights to dwell within our hearts and lives *(see Jn. 14: 15-24)*. What amazing grace! What a privilege!

3. THE COMMUNION OF THE HOLY SPIRIT

Christian living is more than correct doctrine. It includes the experience of 'tasting' that 'the Lord is good' *(see Ps. 34: 8)*. It involves life-transforming personal trust. The Holy Spirit brings life, holiness and lasting happiness to dead sinners. He enlightens our minds, purifies our hearts and energises our wills. It is through the Holy Spirit's gracious ministry that we understand the Scriptures and trust personally in Christ. Through His personal influence—remember He is a person, not an impersonal force *(see Acts 5: 3; Eph. 4: 30)*—we have union and communion with the Father and the Son. Since Christ has removed the guilt of sin, it is the Spirit's work to remove its power and pollution within our souls. We cannot trust Christ *and* love sin (see *2 Cor. 6: 14*). So, 'Hate sin and love this Saviour' said Richard Baxter. Indeed, loving God must produce hatred for sin (see *1 Pet. 1: 15-16*). In all our struggles with 'the world, the flesh and the devil', the 'lust for holiness' will drive away all sinful lust (see *Jas. 4: 1-6,* esp. *v. 6*). The victory of grace is assured if we 'submit to God', seeking both pardon from Christ and purity from the Holy Spirit (see *Jas. 4: 8*). Both are necessary for salvation (see *Heb. 12: 14*). 'Easy-believeism' and 'painted grace' will never save! "From all such delusion, good LORD deliver us!"

CONCLUSION

Paul was thus persuaded that only with the Triune blessing would the chaotic Corinthian and Galatian churches ever know the reality and joys of salvation. We must be persuaded of this in our equally chaotic 21st century. Accordingly Philip Doddridge wrote: 'How often has this comprehensive benediction been pronounced! Let us study it more and more; that we may value it proportionably, that we [pastors and people] set ourselves to *deliver*, or to *receive* it, with becoming solemnity; with eyes and hearts lifted up to God, who, when 'out of Zion he commands the blessing', bestows in it 'life for evermore' [Ps. 133: 3]. Amen!' May this be the assured and joyful faith which inspires not only our Lord's Day worship but every day of our earthly pilgrimage:

Glory to God, the Lord Almighty,
Praise Father, Son and Spirit, One;
We join to celebrate your mercy
And all the wonders you have done!
Father, we worship and adore you,
Likewise the Saviour, Son divine,
Now, through the Spirit who reveals you,
Come, Triune Lord, upon us shine!

(ACC)

BELIEVE THE GOSPEL OF JESUS CHRIST

The Gospel of John, Chapter 1

29 The next day John [the Baptist] saw Jesus coming toward him, and said, "Behold! The Lamb of God who takes away the sin of the world!"

The Gospel of John, Chapter 3

16 "For God so loved the world that He gave His only begotten Son, that whoever believes in Him should not perish but have everlasting life."

ABIDE IN CHRIST

The Gospel of John, Chapter 15

I AM the true vine, and My Father is the vinedresser.
2 "Every branch in Me that does not bear fruit He takes away; and every *branch* that bears fruit He prunes, that it may bear more fruit.

3 "You are already clean because of the word which I have spoken to you.

4 "Abide in Me, and I in you. As the branch cannot bear fruit of itself, unless it abides in the vine, neither can you, unless you abide in Me.

5 "I am the vine, you *are* the branches. He who abides in Me, and I in him, bears much fruit; for without Me you can do nothing.

6 "If anyone does not abide in Me, he is cast out as a branch and is withered; and they gather them and throw *them* into the fire, and they are burned.

7 "If you abide in Me, and My words abide in you, you will ask what you desire, and it shall be done for you.

8 "By this My Father is glorified, that you bear much fruit; so you will be My disciples.

WALK IN THE HOLY SPIRIT

Paul's Letter to the Galatians, Chapter 5

14 For all the law is fulfilled in one word, *even* in this: "You shall love your neighbour as yourself."

15 But if you bite and devour one another, beware lest you be consumed by one another!

16 I say then: Walk in the Spirit, and you shall not fulfill the lust of the flesh.

17 For the flesh lusts against the Spirit, and the Spirit against the flesh; and these are contrary to one another, so that you do not do the things that you wish.

18 But if you are led by the Spirit, you are not under the law.

19 Now the works of the flesh are evident, which are: adultery, fornication, uncleanness, lewdness,

20 idolatry, sorcery, hatred, contentions, jealousies, outbursts of wrath, selfish ambitions, dissensions, heresies,

21 envy, murders, drunkenness, revelries, and the like; of which I tell you beforehand, just as I also told *you* in time past, that those who practice such things will not inherit the kingdom of God.

22 But the fruit of the Spirit is love, joy, peace, longsuffering, kindness, goodness, faithfulness,

23 gentleness, self-control. Against such there is no law.

24 And those *who are* Christ's have crucified the flesh with its passions and desires.

25 If we live in the Spirit, let us also walk in the Spirit.

26 Let us not become conceited, provoking one another, envying one another.

LIVE THE BLESSED LIFE

The Gospel of Matthew, Chapter 5

And seeing the multitudes, [JESUS] went up on a mountain, and when He was seated His disciples came to Him.

2 Then He opened His mouth and taught them, saying:

3 "Blessed *are* the poor in spirit, For theirs is the kingdom of heaven.

4 Blessed *are* those who mourn, For they shall be comforted.

5 Blessed *are* the meek, For they shall inherit the earth.

6 Blessed *are* those who hunger and thirst for righteousness, For they shall be filled.

7 Blessed *are* the merciful, For they shall obtain mercy.

8 Blessed *are* the pure in heart, For they shall see God.

9 Blessed *are* the peacemakers, For they shall be called sons of God.

10 Blessed are those who are persecuted for righteousness' sake, For theirs is the kingdom of heaven.

11 "Blessed are you when they revile and persecute you, and say all kinds of evil against you falsely for My sake.

12 "Rejoice and be exceedingly glad, for great *is* your reward in heaven, for so they persecuted the prophets who were before you.

13 "You are the salt of the earth; but if the salt loses its flavor, how shall it be seasoned? It is then good for nothing but to be thrown out and trampled underfoot by men.

14 "You are the light of the world. A city that is set on a hill cannot be hidden.

15 "Nor do they light a lamp and put it under a basket, but on a lampstand, and it gives light to all *who are* in the house.

16 "Let your light so shine before men, that they may see your good works and glorify your Father in heaven.